PRISCILLA P. WILLIAMS

Falling
APART WHILE
PIECING MYSELF TOGETHER
BROKENNESS TO WHOLENESS

First printing 2017

ISBN: 978-0-9989799-7-7 (Paperback)

HERHEARTWRITESOPENLY, INC.

Cover Design & Illustration: Mitch Green

To the woman who gave me
a voice to speak, believed
in me more than anyone
else, and loved me in a way
that will always remain
unmatched. This is in
celebration of your life and
in remembrance of you, my
mother, Iris Williams.

For every woman searching for her identity, uncertain of who she is and wondering if she still has something worth offering this world, who has felt broken and a little less than whole after a relationship came to an end, has felt the hurt from being abandoned or rejected by those she trusted and allowed herself to become vulnerable and transparent with; this is for you.

What was beautiful
about her brokenness
and completely falling
apart was her ability
to rebuild herself any
way she chose.

CONTENTS

LET'S TAKE A WALK

Devastation takes place suddenly and shows up un-announced in an untimely and inconvenient manner. You may find yourself at the gate of devastation more than once in your life and more than you're ready to face as someone who may have already been through a lot in the past. So, what do you do when things begin crumbling and your peace becomes destruction? When things are falling apart, and you have no control and nothing to grab ahold of; what do you do? Well, things began falling apart uncontrollably in my life, and in that moment, I learned that even when things have crumbled, God searches through the remains and the rub-ble to rebuild from those very same pieces rather than give up on it all. He doesn't leave behind what He can still use, even when there are signs of unsustainable damage. Time proves why holding on can result in more damage, but even so, there are still parts worth salvaging that have promise written all over them.

Like an unhinged door, I became undone, disconnect-ed, broken, and unaware of what the next steps for my life should be. But I was in desperate need of what felt like total repair. It was over; the relationship I had been in for many

years ended, this time for good. Truthfully, I wasn't ready
for it to end nor accept and face the facts. And that's what
often happens after a relationship ends, isn't it? You feel lost,
broken, and completely unaware of where to begin again or
where to start in sorting out the broken pieces of your now
shattered life. But there was a stirring inside of me. I had
reached a place where I longed for change, and the only way
change was going to happen was by first recognizing that
I needed it. The truth is sometimes difficult to face, especially when you cringe thinking of the god-awful truth that
you have been avoiding for some time that has now arrived
and is confronting you directly. This truth requires answers,
answers that result in an effective change when you are authentic and honest with yourself.

I struggled to let go of this relationship. I asked myself
why, why now, and why after so long? But the truth is our
relationship was over. We wanted similar things, but the
time frame in which it would have been reasonable for it to
happen had come and gone. We had walked this same path
together and put in immeasurable time to make sure that it
would work, only to come to a crossroads and realize that

we were going in two entirely different directions. He wasn't ready for what I was ready for. I desired marriage, and he felt he wasn't as ready as I was. Even our faith walk was different. And I vividly remember the times I heard the voice of the Lord whisper, "How can two walk together if they don't agree?" God had been tugging on the strings of my heart that entire time, yet I ignored His voice countless times. I can't even begin to tell you how often I minimalized His voice and tried applying it to the disagreements he and I would have rather than accepting it was purely the fact that our walk in Faith was different, amongst other things, and it was time for us to part ways. My life as I knew it began crumbling, and I desperately held on to whatever I could. I found myself fighting to piece myself together as I was falling apart in the midst of emotional chaos. Things can get a little out of hand when we try to control the direction for our life or the outcome of something unexpected, and how things began unfolding wasn't quite how I had expected them to.

Has there been a tugging on your heart lately?

Right before you answer this question, I want you to unmask and be completely honest with yourself. If you don't want to keep going back to what's familiar and what you have known for so long, you must understand a few things. You see, you will never be able to overcome what you are unwilling to confront; remaining bound to something holds you captive and stops you from moving forward. Many times, it's hard to recognize this because you have become so used to it, so it somehow doesn't resonate as something that needs to be changed.

What you will find as you continue to read are some hard truths that even I myself avoided, most times intentionally. I invite you to take this walk with me, but before you do, I want you to ask yourself:

- Am I ready for change?
- How do I know it's time for change?
- How long have I been dealing with this same circumstance no matter how many times I've confronted it before?
- Am I looking for a temporary or permanent and effective change?

Grab ahold of my hand and hold tight. Allow me to remove my mask first—the mask of shame I wore at one point in my life—as I open up and share my heart with you. Not only do I offer you my heart, but I offer you my vulnerability, my transparency, and my truth.

Often, we are told that we have a choice, but how often do you find yourself making the right one? Is there a right or wrong choice? And how do you know for sure? It is my hope and heart's prayer that as you embark on this journey with me, you will begin to not only see yourself throughout my story but that you will find yourself—find who *YOU* are. I was given a choice, and uncertain of which path to take, I chose the one that seemingly felt right to me. On that path, I quickly became disappointed and began to get frustrated, wondering why things weren't working out as I wanted them to. That was the problem; it was all about me. I didn't consider God's will for my life, and quite frankly, I wrote Him out of my plans, feeling I had better control of things if I did it my way. Nevertheless, God quickly reminded me after seeing so many of my shortcomings that He had not let me go but wanted to know whether I would trust Him again.

Trusting was something I had been struggling and having difficulty with, even with people I could physically touch and see, and now I'm being asked to trust someone I haven't seen? But what did I have to lose? I'd had a relationship with God at one point in my life, and somewhere along the lines, I became lost and got disconnected from Him. I am reminded that just as I was lost on the path I chose, God didn't forget about me; He remained connected to me the entire time. He found me wandering and convicted my heart by reminding me of where He had already brought me, time and time again, up until that day. And it would prove why I vowed to never let Him go again.

LEARNING

I find myself still learning how to separate what I know from what I feel, and to be quite honest, from time to time, this happens to be one of the few things I still struggle with. I'll admit that, at times, I allow my emotions to get carried away—sometimes to the point of no return. It's like taking a long walk to a destination, and once you finally arrive, you realize that where you were going is different and has naturally been altered. Say it has now become a ledge. What would you do? Would you turn around and leave? Or would you look for another route? Most would turn around and leave or find another route. But for me, well, I jump. At that point, there is no turning back because I have already come too far.

For nearly a year, I allowed myself to drown and get completely lost in my emotions after the ending of a relationship I had been in for many years. I had thought I would be with him for the rest of my life. We didn't go through anything that other couples don't experience; it's just that I thought we could get through everything, as we usually did. But with time, it reached a point where we both knew one of us would eventually have to let go. It was clear we were at our end, and no matter what we did, what we tried, or what we discussed repeatedly, there wasn't going to be an effective change that would keep us together.

It wasn't until after our relationship ended that I began to discover who I am. I guess I thought I knew who I was, but how could I when I'd spent so much time drowning myself in someone else, entirely forgetting me? Therefore, that's where I will begin.

I always had a heart for putting the needs of others before mine, even if that meant sacrificing my happiness. I believed that if the needs of others were met before mine were, then I was doing something good, and in essence, I believed they would, in return, do the same for me without my having to ask. Little did I know that what I did for others wouldn't mean they would do the same for me, but that it would lead to me having to ask—more times than I expected and more times than it was voluntarily given to me. What a painful lesson this was for me. Now, don't get me wrong, putting the needs of others before your own isn't a bad thing, and I never saw it that way. But putting someone else's needs before mine without my own needs ever being met left me depleted and with less than complete peace of mind. I learned quickly after our relationship ended that I felt like I was on my last leg emotionally, mentally, spiritually and in everything else that meant me being at my best. It felt like I had very little left and nothing left to give.

I was devastated, yet I became liberated. It was what I needed in order to begin my journey towards my truth. No one knew that our relationship had ended, and as a matter of fact, it wasn't even discussed or spoken about. The truth is, I was embarrassed, and quite frankly, I didn't want to speak with anyone about it. I feared being bombarded with a barrage of questions that usually follow a break-up. Not only was I embarrassed, but I was also hurt.

I was hurt so badly that I spent months on end dwelling in the pain of my choices and decisions that hadn't resulted in a ring or the wedding that my heart desired and longed for. Here I was, no ring and no marriage, just me. I spent many years of my life with someone only to find myself where I had been prior to meeting him, alone.

It's me; I am left with only me. Four walls and me, filled with silence. The kind of silence that screamed at me with guilt and blame, telling myself over and over again that I wasn't enough and that it was my fault, my fault I was alone, by myself again. Telling myself that I was not worth it because if I were, I would be planning a wedding instead of picking up all these broken pieces after he left, pieces of me. I had fallen apart, and I was trying to piece myself back together.

When God is trying to get your attention, I believe He starts gently and subtly, but after a time of constantly ignoring Him, His messages become more obvious and almost earth-shattering. It's clear to me now that God had, had enough of watching my stumbles and falls, and He was ready to set me free despite what I felt was a need to hold on.

God went about everything gracefully rather than dev-astatingly, and it started with people who were dear to me and whom I called my friends at that time. That in itself was tough. I mean, how do you let go of long-time friendships and relationships you've built over the years?

How? Well, that part of trusting God's plan and will for my life, knowing that He knew what would be better for me despite all the things I told myself, was where I needed to put my trust. Trusting what I knew at that point over what I felt. Knowing that God's plan was sure, and whatever I was feeling about that separation from those friendships would hurt, but the hurt would be temporary.

Not only would trusting what I knew more than what I felt be necessary then, but the truest test would come when it became time to close the door and say goodbye once and for all to the person I shared many years of my life with. I didn't know why then, and it wasn't until recently that I saw it completely clearly. You see, I told myself he was it. To me, there was no letting go and no starting over. If I was going to ride the waves and hold tight, he was the one it would be with. But little did I know that God had so much more for me, more than I was continually choosing for myself for so long.

I wrestled back and forth for some time with why I held on for as long as I did. What was it that kept me there and why didn't I walk away sooner, even after I became aware that it was time to do so? Knowing that I had an out and that my Heavenly Father was calling me back to Him? Of course, there was a reason—there was a reason I held on, just as anyone else would. I loved him. I loved him with my whole heart. I began narrowing it down to specifically why. While he and I were together, he helped me in ways that even I didn't realize until long after our relationship ended. He complimented me countless times throughout our relationship, and even then, I still didn't see myself the way he saw me and felt I

"If I am all these things he proclaimed, then why was I still without a ring?"

still needed even more reassurance. He would continually remind me of the beauty he saw in me, both externally and internally, aspects of myself that, to me, were not as favorable. But despite his attempts, it would ultimately be up to me to see in myself what he saw. Him seeing my beauty would never be enough if it wasn't something I could see on my own without his words of affirmation.

The fact that I needed to hear those words were, in fact,my desperate cry for self-love. Internally, *my inner self ached* to be loved, acknowledged, complimented, and admired by none other than myself first. Talk about a cry for help, while all along, he was helping me to see something I was completely oblivious and blind to. It had to begin with me.

It's also why, at times, it was difficult for me to accept all the beautiful things he would say to me as the truth. Difficult because *if I am all these things he proclaimed, then why was I still without a ring?* Knowing what I know now that I didn't know then would unlock all the answers to my questions, many questions I had to seek the truth behind in order to know more about.

When it's time to make a change in your life with regard to something or someone, when it's time to let go and close that chapter once and for all, you'll find yourself wrestling between the desire to hold on and the desire to let go. This could be walking away from an unhealthy or less than desirable relationship, choosing a different or new career path, abandoning and leaving behind old habits, ending less than meaningful friendships, or anything that requires the act of separating—the truth is, it can be tough.

THE MESSENGER

One afternoon, a friend and I were out having lunch together—after having to reschedule several times for one reason or another due to the busyness of life. We hadn't seen each other for some time and had been planning for this day, so it felt good to finally get together as girlfriends to catch up, talk, and find out what was going on in each other's lives. Our conversations usually surrounded discussions about family, life, career, relationships, and future goals or plans that either of us may have had. It was always a time for enlightenment and encouragement that left us both refreshed and filled. As we were nearing the end of our lunch and wrapping up our conversation, a young woman who works at the restaurant approached our table and asked if she could have a seat by me. Although I found it odd because I did not know her and was quite hesitant, I welcomed her and said yes. The words that would follow shortly after she began to speak would ultimately alter the rest of my life from that day forward.

Initially, I could see that she was very nervous and timid but was also determined to tell me whatever it was that had led her to our table. She introduced herself and went on to say that she passed our table on several occasions in a hurry, trying to avoid coming over because it was something she had never done before, but God kept leading her back to our table because He had a message for me that she had to deliver. She then asked me if it was OK for her to share with me what she had to share. I was slightly hesitant and may have been just as nervous as her, if not more so, but aware of the power and ability of God, I said yes.

Once she began to speak, I listened attentively to her first set of words which were, "God wants you to know that when you cry, He cries, and when you hurt, He hurts and that He loves you and is able to give and show you the love you deserve if you could just trust Him." She went on to share a few more things, which included some very personal details I had never shared with anyone. After she was done speaking, I began crying and remember looking at my friend in complete disbelief that this had just taken place. I know I wasn't the only one in disbelief as I looked at my friend, who said, "Girl, only you know; only you know."

Moments later, the young woman stepped away from

our table but returned shortly thereafter with a folded piece
of paper that she handed me. It was her name and number;
she said she wanted to invite me to her church, and that if I
didn't know Christ or have a relationship with Him, He was
ready to be a Father to me and show me the true meaning of
love. She then hugged and embraced me, excused herself,
and left.

I was left in awe, and it wasn't
because I didn't believe what she said but
because unless you knew me personally
and I shared details with you, there was
absolutely no way anyone would have
known the personal details she shared

"What broke me couldn't mend me."

with me. Isn't it something that even when we know what's
right and we have an out, we still choose to go against that
and tell ourselves "I've got this" and, "I know what to do," yet
the only thing that does is bury us deeper than we are able
to sustain ourselves on our own? Well, even after having that
encounter and knowing it was time to obey God and allow
Him to do His will for my life, I chose, against my better judg-
ment, to continue writing my own story, which meant I would

stay in the relationship I was in, holding on for as long as I could, trying to fix it and doing whatever I could possibly do to not let it go. In my mind, I thought I could make that happen. I felt that if we'd been together that long, why wouldn't it work? Why couldn't what was broken be mended? But the truth is, *what broke me couldn't mend me.*

Here's what I learned about holding on. *Holding on can go either way. You can continually hurt yourself time and time again, where eventually, even though things might ultimately change and lead to your heart's desire, you'd still be out of God's will and plan for your life.* On the other hand, you can be obedient to God's call and will for your life, ceasing all hurt and pain or avoiding it all together. Overall, change starts with you.

You see, it wasn't that holding on was a bad thing; it was because that was not what God had in mind for me. He had so much more in store for me than what I was fighting so hard to hold on to, and it doesn't take away from the person I was holding on to or myself, it's just that God longed for something different. He desired more from me, more out of me, and even had so much more to teach me that I needed to learn. God knew me well, better than I knew myself, and He wasn't going to allow me to stay. I went home that day after leaving the restaurant, replaying in my mind what had just happened and how much of it I did not want to be true. I wished it had never happened, and I desired for things to remain as they were because my heart was willing to fight and hold on until it became everything I wanted.

I held on. I held on for dear life. At that point, there was no way I was willing to start over. I mean why? Why after so long? Why after so much? Why? But I couldn't wish it away. At that time, I didn't understand the why, but as I write these words, it's clearer now.

I'd had the Jonah experience. If you may recall, in the Bible, Jonah ran from God. But why did Jonah run? Jonah ran out of fear and an unwilling heart to do what he was commanded to do by God. In doing so, he made matters worse and harder for himself because God's will, regardless of Jonah's fears and objections, still had to be done. Jonah had been given specific instructions that required him to do something he did not want to do. Jonah was disobedient and ran, but God didn't let up or change his mind about what he needed Jonah to do. God pursued Jonah relentlessly, and although it still came with a struggle, Jonah reconsidered and fulfilled what he was supposed to do initially. God's mercy was shown to Jonah because God is gracious and merciful to us even when we are undeserving because we've disobeyed Him. Which leads me to ask, what has God commanded you to do that you aren't doing or haven't done yet?

We doubt ourselves too easily. We don't give ourselves enough credit, and we can often feel that we are incapable of doing more or, more importantly, being more and receiving more. Therefore, we limit ourselves and, in doing so, limit God.

For the next several months, I chose to hold on and give my all, but it didn't give me the feeling of peace I was searching for. As a matter of fact, it instead became more uncomfortable. Uncomfortable to the point that what had been bearable before was no longer bearable. Even the littlest of things didn't seem quite so little anymore. Eventually, he and

I mutually agreed to part ways. No hate, no animosity, and no regrets. Just valuable lessons learned, and admiration with love from what we experienced together that would help us both grow as individuals wherever our lives would take us from that day forward.

PIECES

And there I was with all my
broken pieces in my hand
shattered, broken, and torn
apart still picking up pieces
after you left trying to piece
myself back together again
because of my desire to be
whole.

THE BREAKING

Where do you begin after heartbreak, or the devastation of the less-than-expected has shown up at your front door, uninvited? What do you do when you don't know what to do? Who do you turn to? And do they have the answers you'll need to make it all better or just temporary words of comfort? These were the questions I found myself pondering in my heart because I felt broken and was filled with sorrow. I was left with all these pieces, to figure out how I was going to put myself back together again and where I was going to begin. I believed I could make it right and that I could somehow fix myself and feel whole again. I didn't seek help because I felt I had all the answers and could find the peace I longed for if I just gave myself the time to navigate through all those raw emotions.

But I was wrong, and for a long time, I didn't feel any better. For months on end, I held on to the memories and pieces of my past with hopes that it could be mended. In doing so, I chose not to begin my healing process.

There were nights I fell asleep with tears streaming down my face like a leaking faucet in desperate need of repair. My body would rest, but my mind wasn't rested. I was fueled by how hurt I was. Not the kind of hurt with the need for vengeance, but a kind of hurt that became a friend to me. I invited it in and allowed it to comfort me—it was an excuse for me to not let go. It was a way of blaming myself and finding fault within as I told myself repeatedly that I was again single and alone because I wasn't enough for anyone, and I would have to accept that even if I didn't want to.

So, that's what I did; I accepted it, all the while again forgetting who God was and failing to put my trust in Him to mend me and make me whole. There would be so much for me to learn, and this was just the tip of the iceberg.

Now I want to take some time to unpack brokenness, because it doesn't only happen when relationships come to an end. Brokenness occurs at the site of heartbreak, but many other things can lead to a broken heart, and a lot of times, when you hear the word broken, the two are easily associated. Brokenness can be caused by the devastating news of the loss of a loved one, or it can be caused in a child witnessing their parents, whom they've seen together for their whole lives, parting ways. Relocating from one place to another and having difficulty readjusting to a new normal, the result of rejection, abandonment, and disappointment, can also lead to brokenness. Other things that might lead to brokenness are the feelings of emptiness or feeling unfulfilled in one area or more of your life, which can also lead to depression. All of these things are emotionally tied together and are directly connected to your heart.

"I was broken but worthy enough to be God's vessel."

I began longing to feel whole again as brokenness became too painful and felt like a heavy burden. It left me in a place where I was unsettled because the love I gave wasn't received the way I felt it should have been or reciprocated the way my heart desired. With time, I would find the beauty in my brokenness and how that gave God room to do amazing things in and through my life. I was broken but worthy enough to be God's vessel. Yes, worthy! And that's what I want you to see. Even now, in your brokenness, you are powerful and can become more so when you allow God to heal and transform you into something that will result in a stronger and greater you! Now, pause for a moment and find the beauty in your brokenness despite how difficult or painful it may be to sort through the shards. Recognize your worthiness, because you *are* worthy.

Moving from brokenness to wholeness is a decision; you have to want it. It's your way of saying, "I no longer want to be this way. I no longer have a desire to feel this way, and I'm ready to be whole again." It's your declaration: "I want the pain to cease. I no longer want to hurt. I want to exchange my discomfort for comfort, and I am yearning for the peace I had before this uninvited disruption came in and wrecked my life." This means exchanging your broken pieces for peace with the Master healer, The One who can mend your broken heart, make you whole again, and take you from brokenness to wholeness, creating a masterpiece through you. It's time to hand over your pieces.

DAMAGED GOODS

I felt damaged, and it became easy for me to feel that no one would want me. I questioned if I would ever be good enough and whether or not I had something worth fighting for. It was in that moment that I began to see myself as irreparably damaged goods. I felt that no one else would ever want me, and even if they did, it would ultimately lead to the relationship ending. Doubt began creeping in like a thief in the night who found a hiding place and nestled comfortably in my mind. I had already told myself after hitting what seemed to be the same dead-end wall over and over again that I would only be good enough for some things, but never enough for everything I felt and knew I deserved.

"I felt like a complete failure all around."

This feeling lingered and resided with me for a while as I considered how long I'd spent in one relationship that had failed. I felt like a complete failure all around—a failure because if it didn't work and we were no longer together, then that meant total failure to me.

Now, let's have a moment of truth. Ask yourself who embraces failure easily? I'll be the first to say certainly not I, and that opened the door to even more doubt. Many questions filled my mind. Questions such as who would want me? Who would want to accept me as their own, become one with me, and build with me? Amongst other plagues of doubt, things began to fester and settle in quickly. In my mind, I thought no one would want me now. To me, I felt it was the end of ever discovering the possibility of love again, despite the promise God made to me. I was still choosing to short-change myself by filling my mind with negative thoughts and feelings. Consequently, I allowed my past to predict my future even though I had much ahead of me that I could not see.

But God knew, and He allowed me to remain that way until I chose to finally take my hand off the steering wheel of my life and allow Him to regain control. I mean, I had got it wrong for so long and so many times, I felt there was no way it would ever be right.

I thought I knew what I was doing. I wanted my life to be the way I had imagined it would be and with whom I wanted, and that's where I lost control. Thinking that way caused me to stray further away from God's will for my life, and is why it just wasn't ever going to work and didn't. During the time of feeling this way, still in my brokenness, the only option I gave myself and rationalized as reasonable, which brought me temporary comfort and allowed me to not let go completely at first, was to tell myself that our relationship was repairable. I told myself that with enough time apart, just maybe we could make it work again.

> *"I didn't want to start over, meet someone new, or have to relearn someone."*

At that point, he was living his life, and I was, too. I was certain that given enough time apart, we'd naturally do what I saw others do and what we ourselves had done during those years—we would get back together soon. I still felt God would bring us back together; he would be the man I want, I would be the woman he wants, and we would be together. I would still be able to have my heart's desires fulfilled.

Still yet, I was wrong. That was not part of God's will for my life, and the end actually meant the end. I still held tightly to hurt and un-forgiveness and thought it could all be fixed in this relationship.

The truth is, I didn't want to start over, meet someone new, or have to relearn someone and go through what seems like a whole process again. Getting to know someone happens over time and takes years. You don't get to know someone in a short span of time, although you can in some ways determine their intentions. Even then, as you are both growing and evolving together, you are individually discovering and becoming who you truly are. Whether that was what I wanted or not, it was time to let go.

Everyone's path is different, and our experiences can be similar yet go in different directions. It was time for me to choose a different path—one other than the one I had chosen countless times before in my past.

Damaged and alone, damaged and in a relationship, damaged and barely holding on, damaged and fighting to feel whole again—just damaged. Can you identify with any of these? And is this how you feel even now? You're not alone. Being damaged doesn't make you irreparable, it makes you a vessel. *Damaged is not your final destination.* I know what feeling damaged is like, and I can imagine how it feels for you. I felt unworthy. I felt undeserving. I felt damaged.

> *"Even with unsustainable damage I was still worthy."*

But the truth is, even with unsustainable damage, I was still worthy, and so are you. God did not look down on me or condemn me for the choices I made that led to how damaged I felt or my brokenness. Instead, He was patient enough to see me through from the heartbreak to my full recovery and complete emotional wholeness. And if you allow Him, He will do the very same for you as well. God is more concerned about where you're going than where you've been. He's not going through the pages of your past shaking His head in disappointment. Rather, He's certifying you based on your experience because it qualifies you to make an impact and difference in someone else's life.

GET IT RIGHT

She wanted to get it right with him. Starting over was never a part of her plan. The thought of having to be vulnerable to someone new when she'd spent years giving that to one, the one she thought would have her forever, pierced her heart even more. Although she understood that there would be times when things would have to end, she never thought it would be between herself and him.

HOLDING ON TO HEARTBREAK

Heartbreak is difficult, and it takes time to get to a place where you are ready to let go of the hurt. We hold on because it becomes easier to cling to the memories of our past. This goes back to familiarity, and here's what we hold on to: we hold on to the pictures taken together and of each other, the letters, texts, and greeting cards exchanged back and forth. The dates that occurred and places traveled to, the time spent with each other and their family, friends, and so forth. You get a bit wrapped up in it all, and it's a lot to let go of, isn't it? It only becomes harder the longer you hold on to these memories you collected that are no longer there or a part of your now.

Sound familiar? This was my exact struggle, and I eventually came to call it holding on to heartbreak. Holding on, for me, was me holding on to the thoughts of being in a relationship again with this man I'd spent years of my life with. I didn't want to think about having to start over or begin again. It was my cop-out and my way of telling anyone who was interested in pursuing me that I was not yet ready or open to anything new because my heart had not yet healed. Nor was I ready to move on.

For a while, it worked, and I held on to the memories from my past of what could be for just about a year after things ended. Then one morning, I woke up and was lying in bed taking in the stillness and quietness of what I call the calm; it was peaceful. Mornings like this, when I'm not in a rush or bound by a schedule that requires me to be some-where by a certain time, are my favorites because usually, I stretch that time for as long as I can, enjoying the small bursts of "laziness" that are short-lived anyway for one rea-son or another.

While lying there that morning, I heard a firm, but re-assuring, voice say, "It is time for your healing process to be done." Immediately, I became defensive, responding, "Huh ... what?" I didn't understand what exactly that had to do with me, because again, in my heart, that's not what I wanted to do, and I just wasn't ready. I even tried dismissing it, but, again, I heard the same voice say, "It is time for your healing process to be done."

As much as I wanted to go back and forth, debating what I heard or asking again, I decided to accept what I'd heard, knowing it was the voice of the Lord and that truthfully, it was time to let go of my past and the memories I so easily identified with and found immediate comfort in.

Honestly, I was holding myself back and wasn't growing or moving forward as people usually do after going through the motions of heartbreak. I created excuses and felt sorry for myself because of familiarity. Familiarity for me meant wanting to stick with what I already knew rather than putting a period on it, closing that chapter, and being open to a new chapter of my life, whatever that may be.

I finally made the decision not to go back and forth but to say instead, "OK, Lord, I am ready to trust you. You've done your part; now it's time to do mine." I gave up my will and decided to put my trust in God's hands. Making that choice was the best decision I've ever made for myself. I look back now and see how things fell immediately into place the moment I decided to let go of heartbreak.

It wasn't as if I was still hurting at that time or that I was angry, sad, or unforgiving. Enough time had passed, almost a year to be exact, and I had forgiven myself and all the hurt by that time. So, truthfully, I wasn't hurting anyone but myself, tainting all the possibilities that my future held. When I let go of the hurt, life began again for me.

"Nothing comes as a surprise to God, and He's aware of every one of your needs."

If you are experiencing heartbreak and you feel lost, confused, and have been drowning in your emotions, that's OK. Yes! It's OK. But don't allow yourself to stay there. Don't allow heartbreak to become your comforter and friend, ultimately giving you a reason to hold on to something or someone who has already let go and moved on. Take the time you need to feel, but don't become so immune to it that you become numb to the reality that time is passing by, and the time that you are spending is time you will never get back. I did that, I did that for longer than I needed to, and if it wasn't for God and His calm, still, and quiet voice speaking to me that morning, it is likely that even years later I would still be where I was then.

Just as with the young woman who approached me at the table in the restaurant, I invite you, if you don't know or have a relationship with God, to develop one with Him. He will not only guide you, comfort you, and be a Rock in a weary and lonely place, but He will take your brokenness, heal you, and make you emotionally whole again. Nothing comes as a surprise to God, and He's aware of every one of your needs. Your past, the scars you try to hide, the painful brokenness, hurt, and discomfort, He wants it all and is waiting for you to run into His arms so He can embrace you just as you are. Who you are doesn't scare Him, and He's not shaken by your past.

I cannot promise that you won't have flashbacks from your past or that you won't sometimes cringe over the painful memories you've experienced, but what this means for you is that you will always remember what you overcame, where you were then compared to now, and what you will be able to overcome, no matter what.

This is for any who have experienced heartbreak, brokenness, rejection, your innocence taken away from you by force whether you were a child or adult, abandonment, divorce—no matter what it is, take your broken pieces and give them to God. He wants to restore you from those very same-pieces, heal you, and make you over into a better, stronger, and more resilient you.

I heard a story once about a little girl named Jenny:
Jenny and her mother were at a store one day, and while in the checkout line, Jenny saw a circle of sparkling white pearls. Filled with excitement, Jenny asked her mother, "Please, please, Mom; please, can I have them?"

Her mother told her that if she truly desired the pearls, she would have to save up enough money, which was close to two dollars, to buy them herself.

Once Jenny got home, she emptied her piggy bank to find only seventeen cents. Realizing she was still short the nearly two dollars she would need to buy those pearls, Jenny did a few more chores than she was used to doing and even asked her neighbor if she could pick dandelions from her garden to earn extra money.

Jenny's birthday arrived, and her grandmother gave her a new dollar bill. Finally, she had enough money to buy the pearl necklace. Jenny loved her pearls because they made her feel grown-up—she wore them everywhere.

Jenny also had a very loving father, and every night, he would stop in the middle of whatever he was doing to read her a story. One night, after reading the story, he asked Jenny if she loved him.

"Oh, yes, Daddy," said Jenny. "You know that I love you."

He then asked her for her pearls.

She said, "Oh, Daddy, not my pearls!" and offered him something else in exchange.

Her father said, "That's OK; I love you," as he gave her a goodnight kiss on her cheek.

Some time passed, and one night, again after story time, he asked Jenny, "Do you love me?"

She replied, "Daddy, I love you."

In return, he once more asked for her

pearls.

Jenny said, "Daddy, oh no, not my pearls! But you can-have my baby doll that I recently got for my birthday."

"That's OK," her father said once more as he kissed her goodnight and told her he loves her, as usual.

Several days had passed when Jenny's father came to read her a story again, and this time, Jenny was sitting on her bed. Her lips trembled as she said, "Here, Daddy," and held out her hand. She opened her hand, and there was the pearl necklace she loved so much, nestled inside a box. She released them into her father's hand.

Her father held the plastic pearls with one hand, and with his other hand, he pulled from his pocket a blue velvet box. Inside were beautiful genuine pearls. Jenny's father had, had them all along and was waiting for her to give up the cheap stuff so he could give her the real thing.

— Author unknown

My dear sister, I am compelled to ask you, what are you holding on to? What are you holding yourself back from? Are you willing to miss out on something greater because you want to hold on to what's familiar? Or are you ready to let go? Like Jenny's father, God is waiting for you to let go of your will and cling to His. He has something better for you on the other side of what you choose to hold on to. God is your sustainer, and there is nothing anyone can offer you that He cannot. Stop allowing your worth to be devalued by those who have yet to recognize it. You must ask yourself, "Do I want what's authentic and real,

"You are worth more than holding on to something that's cheap and has no value; you deserve something real and filled with substance"

or are am I OK with the bare minimum?" Then wait for an answer. *You are worth more than holding on to something that's cheap and has no value; you deserve something real and filled with substance.*

THE REVOLVING DOOR

Have you ever found yourself in a situation with someone where no matter what you did or how hard you tried, you could never distance yourself or part ways with them?

It's like you're a revolving door, giving them continual access to your life even while knowing how unhealthy and toxic this connection is for you. I've been there, and honestly, as much as I have wished I had let go of these types of connections much sooner, remaining connected taught me the things I needed to know. It brought awareness of what I should avoid and look out for in the future.

Why did I keep letting people in? People who had repeatedly proven to only disappoint and let me down one way or another. Why did I keep giving them unrevoked access to my heart? Access that swung back and forth like a door. I created this revolving door, and it would be entirely up to me to recognize and revoke their access. I was guilty of this. When I reflect and look back, I realize there were times in my life when I had given access to people who no longer deserved to have access to my heart. These connections and relationships robbed me of my peace, authentic love, and what I truly deserved, and often, they made me question my worth and left me feeling less than complete.

"I accepted less and was OK with that by telling myself it was just enough because it was something."

I later realized that the reason I chose to stay or remain connected to what wasn't good for me was because of what I lacked inside, and I needed to discover what that was in order to finally let go once and for all. It wasn't easy; the cycle repeated itself, and each time it did, it was because I had not yet discovered my worth, nor did I love myself as I thought I did.

I accepted less and was OK with that by telling myself it was just enough because it was something. Little did I know that the only person I was robbing was myself because I was keeping myself from receiving the love I deserved. Yet somewhere inside of me, I kept rationalizing my own truth until I realized how I was left feeling in the end—completely empty, depleted, and anything but happy. I had no peace; I was alone, feeling everything but love from the ones I poured myself into. How could someone who has someone still feel incredibly lonely and unloved?

As I lived out my life from day to day, I came to know how much God loves me and declares His love without shame or doubt. Then I began to look at how people who

"If God wants great things for me, why would I continue to settle for less than great?"

would say they loved me made me feel. And when I compared the two, I realized there was no way that God's love for me could feel so great, so peaceful, and so comforting, while the "love" I received from those who said they loved me seemed so much less and left me feeling unloved, unwanted, and unappreciated. I knew then that their love wasn't as pure or as genuine as I had thought.

If God wants great things for me, why would I continue to settle for less than great? It was that simple, and it made perfect sense to me that change was necessary and I had to let go of some people.

Pretending to be happy is easy. I smiled even as I was breaking on the inside. And when asked how I was doing, although I was hurting, it became naturally easy to say, "I am good," and to claim that things were great. But after a while, pretending is no longer an option because how you feel on the inside starts showing on the outside. It shows in how you treat others and how you respond to them, especially those closest to you. I knew I wanted something different for myself because I didn't want to keep walking around with emotions that were no good for me. I was sick and tired of feeling what seemed to be constant torture, and I wanted to lash out every chance I was given so that my anger would be justifiable.

Finally, I shut that revolving door for good. The access I had given to people, allowing them to enter into my heart and my feelings, and to have control over my emotions, was now permanently denied.

Holding on feels better, doesn't it? It's what you know, right? And it's similar to going home and, with your key, gaining access to a place where you feel safe. But going home doesn't always ensure your safety. It doesn't assure you that you will find peace and comfort. Peace begins solely with you, and that's how you should treat your heart. Be mindful of who you give permission and access to. *Your heart is your home; it deserves peace.*

When a baby is born, the parents will nurture and keep the child safe until that child becomes old enough to help himself. But even when they are mature enough, parents still want their child to be safe. At some point, the parents will have to let them go and trust that everything they instilled and taught their child is enough to carry them through and keep them safe in their adult life.

As children become adults, they are faced more and more often with choices their parents cannot make for them. Instead, they must choose which life lesson they will apply as their guide. Until then, the parents must model this by making the choices for them.

Why should that be any different from how you guard your heart? When someone hurts you, whether it's intentional or unintentional, you are now aware and get to choose if you will allow that person to still be a part of your life or not.

Now I don't want you to think this means you will avoid every painful situation or that you will never experience heartbreak and your heart will never ache or hurt, because if I were to tell you that, I would be misleading you. However, if you remember anything from this, I want you to keep in mind that *your heart is a home in which a baby dwells.*

Who do you continue to give your heart access to and how do they treat it? Better yet, how do you treat it? The way your heart feels in private is how others will treat it in public.

Did you catch that?

When you are alone and feel inadequate and empty in your heart, there is no way that it will feel better once you give people access to it in that condition. It's important that you do a heart check and ensure your heart is in the right place before allowing access to anyone. This starts with recognizing your heart's cry and not ignoring its constant plea for complete healing, no matter how shattered and broken you may think you are. Remember, you deserve to feel everything that's authentic and true.

BREAKING THE CYCLE

We can all relate to pain. It's a story we have in common at one point or another in our lives that establishes a foundation. It may not necessarily be the same story, but we all have a story nonetheless. And in this same pain, you can discover healing; healing that begins with vulnerability, transparency, and allowing God to walk through your pain with you and heal that hurt. *Breaking a cycle starts with confronting where the pain stems from.* I wanted to identify my pain and why I kept finding myself there time and time again, repeating the same cycles.

> *"Breaking a cycle starts with confronting where the pain stems from."*

Once I found myself at the same place—realizing that I had been giving all of myself to everyone except myself—it broke me, and I was left falling apart. I had to rebuild and rediscover myself; almost like reintroducing myself to the person I lost when I decided to put the care of others before my own. This was difficult because I had to re-identify with myself and trace back to where and when I went wrong. I also noticed that there was a pattern I unknowingly created and that *my desire to be loved was greater than my desire to love myself.*

Through self-discovery, I found that when a previous relationship didn't work out, although I thought I was ready and found closure to move forward, I wasn't. Making a decision like that left me vulnerable

> *"My desire to be loved was greater than my desire to love myself."*

and open to accept whoever was next, whoever was going to make me feel wanted, and therefore, I was willing to do what seemed like anything to keep that and never lose it, no matter what. I subjected myself to the unknown and allowed things to happen that I wouldn't have had I given myself enough time to heal before moving on. More importantly, I would have avoided another broken cycle that only resulted in heartbreak.

It's mind-boggling to me how easy it is to feel as though we have it all together in the relationships and friendships, the people we associate ourselves with, yet be nowhere close to having it all together, even with everything that's been invested and given. But here's what I've learned from that; I learned that what's broken from the beginning isn't going to be whole because I want it to be, especially if it begins on shaky ground. I also learned that sometimes our emotions give a false sense of what our reality is and may have you thinking that where you are and what you're doing is what's best when, in fact, it's not. And that's where I found myself. *I allowed my emotions to subsequently impair my intelligence, causing my choices to be led by what I felt over what I knew.*

Not to take away from the relationship I was in or the friendships I had, but this had to do solely with me. My choices, my decisions, and not being completely who I needed to be for myself while by myself before inviting and welcoming someone new into my life. There were things I needed to recognize and come to a realization about when it concerned this cycle that I had created.

It's a relief when you finally discover something you have been doing for so long that has affected you more than you realized, whether it is good or bad. From that point, you can address it, put a stop to it, or pay closer attention to improve and be better overall. Knowing what I discovered not only made me stop repeating this broken cycle, but I paid closer attention, improved, and became an even a better person to myself. I broke the cycle when I began loving myself the way I wholeheartedly desired to be loved, how God designed me, as a woman, to be loved through the love He gave and showed me.

Had I not learned what I needed to, and had things worked out as I desired, I would have continued in the relationship I was in not knowing who I was and not fully aware of what I had to offer. Not only would I have had to deal with my insecurities and the unawareness of self but there would be pieces of my past left unaddressed that I would unknowingly have kept carrying and dragging into my future. This again reminds me of how God is so strategically careful in what He allows for our lives. At times, I became worried and concerned, even questioning God on why things didn't work out how I wanted them to, and why what I desired had come to an end. I didn't know that it was all a part of His will and plan.

Rest assured, as I was reassured that *we must be persistent in pursuing God's will for our life over our own will,* and realize how important it is to seek Him before we make it our objective to do what pleases us instead. Breaking a cycle is a choice. It's an intentional action where you want something to manifest and make happen. It happens when you make a committed effort to

"We must be persistent in pursuing God's will for our life over our own will."

see it through from start to satisfaction. Where are you right now in your life? Have you found yourself in a cycle that you're uncomfortable in and ready to break out of? Is it a cycle of addiction, where you keep going back and remaining in an abusive or unhealthy relationship? Perhaps you're running from God's calling for your life? Whatever it may be, you have the power to break that cycle. You are in control, and it is time to identify your pain, confront it, and regain your will power. I believe in you!

HEALING WITH A HEART
OF FORGIVENESS

One of the most crucial parts of healing and receiving the closure I needed was forgiveness. Forgiveness began with me. I chose to first forgive myself for every time I chose someone else over myself. It *"Forgiveness requires us to be committed, honest, and intentional."* was a way of saying that I recognized I was neglectful towards the care I deserved and that I am sorry. Then, little by little, it was time to start working on forgiving those outside of myself. It was important to not only forgive myself but of equal importance was forgiving anyone who had hurt me at some point in my life.

Forgiveness is a struggle for many. It often creates a blame game rather than bringing a solution that allows you to let go, begin again, and move forward. Being unforgiving leaves voids, creates crutches, and gives reasons to hold on. On the other hand, forgiveness is like redemption and being set free. You have to ask yourself what's more important, is it me or what happened to me? What happened to you has no power; it is your need to hold on to what happened that gives it *POWER.* Just as wanting to overcome anything else in our life, *forgiveness requires us to be committed, honest, and intentional.*

How I would be treated at any point in my life, would depend solely on how I treated myself first. During one period of my life, I spent a lot of time in seclusion, away from people and my dependency for them. In that time, I found myself discovering everything I felt I'd lost or no longer had—especially peace. I longed for and was determined to have peace of mind again. It was a necessary time, but very agonizing for me because, at times, it felt as though it wasn't happening fast enough. I realized that much of everything I faced, felt, and experienced was needed so once I got back on my feet, I would never find myself in that broken place again. It was like piecing myself back together from all that remained.

Letting go of the idea that we have all the answers and can fix ourselves is important. For me, a great deal of reliance on God, as well as being patient and kind to myself, were necessary. It was similar to a partnership, entrusting His lead and not relying on only myself. *I had to show myself grace, the same grace God shows us.* Had it been solely up to me, I'm unsure of the state of mind I would be in. I also had to change my perspective on how I saw others, because naturally, I placed blame outwardly rather than carefully looking inward at what caused me to make the choices I did that led to the hurt.

This would mean putting a stop to negative thoughts and channeling of negative emotions and ceasing to make myself the target. I spent countless hours repeatedly telling myself that it was my fault, that I was the reason I was in that destitute, lonely, and broken place. All of these things were happening at once, alongside having to function during everyday responsibilities,

> *"Every day that passed in which I honored my hurt and pain more than I recognized my need for healing, the more broken I became."*

responsibilities that couldn't be shelved until I felt whole again. I want to be honest; there were days I didn't want to fight for my wholeness. There were mornings where I would wake up feeling like everything was continually crumbling inside no matter how much I fought for my healing. It felt like a disaster was taking place within, yet I would leave my home and face the world with a vibrant smile. But hidden just behind that, I was falling apart. I wore this face well, day in and day out, month after month, until I became used to it.

Every day that passed in which I honored my hurt and pain more than I recognized my need for healing, the more broken I became. But regardless of all the emotions that were spiraling out of control inside of me, I mustered up enough strength to continue fighting for myself. I would return home at the end of my day, and pain would greet me at my front door, inviting me in and reminding me of my unattended gaping wounds and hurt. How many of us are guilty of these same cycles and patterns? Of wearing a mask and being a *pretender*, not authentically representing who we are? How many of us find ourselves wandering—searching for peace in our broken and lonely place?

Well, naturally, I became a pretender; it was easy to hide my scars, wounds, and bruises while displaying happiness. I was ready to stop this unhealthy behavior and choose my healing and forgiveness at once. It was just too tiring to hold on to it any longer.

Healing looks different for everyone, and it starts differently, too. For some, it may mean confronting the pain directly, while for others, it starts with forgiveness even when there is no apology received. And this part of it can be tough;

not receiving an apology that you know you deserve, right? I know it's difficult. I haven't received apologies from a lot of people who have hurt me in my past, who left me in a place of brokenness and had no intention of looking back, but I

"My willingness to let go of my hurt granted my heart the peace it was searching and longing for."

forgave them anyway. I found the peace I was looking for in God when I brought my pain to Him and said, "God, I can no longer carry this heavy load; please take it from me, please." And He did. *My willingness to let go of my hurt granted my heart the peace it was searching and longing for.* If you find yourself in a place where you are in a cycle of self-blame, it's time to stop—regardless of how much your own decisions are responsible or if it's entirely what someone else did to you, whether you allowed it or not, gave access or not, granted permission or not. You don't deserve to blame yourself any longer. You are chosen, and you are still worthy even after everything you have gone through and overcome. What you have experienced is not an indictment but rather a testimony of your survival. You survived. You survived things you thought you never would, and that makes you an overcomer. You are so brave!

HER HEART

Her heart has been wound-
ed, bruised, scarred, torn,
broken, and even ripped
apart. It's been battered; it's
been manipulated, used, and
has felt hurt and pain. But
her soul still loves. My God,
it still loves, and her heart
remains authentic and true.

COURAGE

Courage is exhibiting

love again after being

hurt countless times.

MY REFLECTION

It took some time for me to learn how to completely love myself for how God created me and who I was—a lot of time. It was years before I completely accepted every inch of myself, and it didn't happen until recently. So yes, this meant even while I was in a relationship, I didn't see myself the way how I see myself now. For many years, for as long as I could remember, I dealt with different types of insecurities that made me feel less than, not enough, and unwanted, no matter how many times I had been told that I am beautiful, gorgeous, or pretty. It was something I didn't believe, and in some ways, I felt had to do with the desires of my heart being still left unfulfilled.

What I wanted and my reality didn't align. I wanted a committed covenant marriage and to be living the life I imagined and pictured in my mind by a certain time. Because, again, if I am this smart, beautiful, gorgeous, and grounded woman filled with wisdom, then what was I missing? How could I be enough yet not enough to commit to for life? Little did I know it would begin with accepting how I saw myself first, not how others saw or viewed me; not even their opinions would carry this type of precedence. I had to face the woman who stood before the mirror, the reflection that looked back at me. It was me versus me and nobody else. *The mirror reflected my outward beauty, but securely hid my insecurities and internal scars.*

I began taking a look at every part of myself; including the parts I had disliked and despised for years and decided to accept that those parts I didn't like so much would be a part of me forever. There would be no removing or replacing them. Instead of seeing these parts of myself in a negative light, I started seeking what was beautiful about them and how uniquely, creatively, and carefully designed I was by God. And I found security in this new-found confidence of self-love.

> *"The mirror reflected my outward beauty, but securely hid my insecurities and internal scars."*

God chose me and made me in His likeness, what He saw as beauty as opposed to what I saw as unattractive and not so pretty. I embraced Priscilla and everything that came with her: all of my scars, my pain, my emotions, my past, my choices. I accepted that it is all of those things that make me who I am today, the woman standing *"My soul craved* before the mirror. I no longer wanted *to be loved by me,* to be a beautiful face without any *the very soul I* depth or substance inside. What a *had neglected."* moment that was for me. My soul craved to be loved by me, the very soul I had neglected for so long—self-love, self-worth, the discovery of myself, and most importantly, an intimate relationship with God. His daughter, myself, had been knocking on the gates of my heart for so long and I could no longer ignore it.

Letting go of all the things I'd held on to for so long felt good. No longer could anyone else, no matter how hard they tried, point out something that I wasn't already aware of and found peace and closure with. No longer would I give them a chance to use those things against me. There were countless times I walked swiftly past the mirror to avoid what I needed to address. Facing myself in the mirror wasn't only about what could be seen externally anymore but was about the things that could not be seen, my hidden wounds, scars, bruises, and my unaddressed brokenness. All of these things tied into how I felt, including feeling like I was never enough.

Not feeling like you're enough stems from insecurities, and it's something that many of us face as women. It can be the smallest detail that no one else but us notices or is aware of. A detail that, even if it is noticed, is found to be minimal and still beautiful in the eyes of others. It's important to keep in mind that insecurities aren't just physical, but can be mental too. A mind filled with self-doubt, self-hate, lack of confidence, and the inability to live your life in passionate pursuit of your goals and career weighs heavily in the same lines of insecurities. It's a state of feeling less than completely secure in one area or another. Nevertheless, it doesn't take away from who you are, as you were created whole in the likeness of God. It takes a peeling away of self to truly discover your worth beyond your reflection in the mirror. *With all my layers peeled back, I began discovering my worth.*

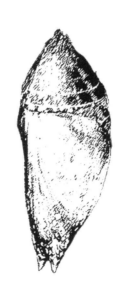

DISCOVERING MY WORTH

After finally addressing the things I battled with, both externally and internally, bit by bit, I realized that I had always been enough; I just needed to see it for myself first and then love myself the way God loves me. God looked past all the things I saw as hindrances and reasons not to be loved but still loved me unconditionally. I was tired of pretending, and *the moment I discovered my worth was liberating*. It freed me from the masks that I wore and the shadows I hid behind. It didn't mean I thought I was better than anyone else or that no one deserved to be a part of my life, but it meant that I was going to be a lot wiser and even more careful about whom I let my guard down with or vulnerable and transparent to.

> *"God looked past all the things I saw as hindrances and reasons not to be loved but still loved me unconditionally."*

We live in a time where we want to have a sense of connection and find something we share in common with another person, but how easy is it to do this, really, when your mind only reminds you of your past poor choices and your mistakes? Getting there means truly first getting it right. It doesn't mean that things are going to be perfect all the time, but for me, it meant that any time I found myself in a place that made me feel uncomfortable or like I was being taken advantage of, that person would have a first-class ticket to fly out of my life for good.

I was no longer willing to subject myself to things that made me feel uncomfortable, things that made me feel un-happy, or things that took away my peace or robbed me of my joy. It meant loving and caring for myself in the way I knew I deserved in order for me to, in return, receive it back. After all, if this is the only life that I'm given to live, every single day until my breath has left my body, why would I want to be subjected to something that is less than what makes me feel good? Undoubtedly, there will be things we are unable to avoid, while there are other things that we can choose to NOT be a part of JUST because they're familiar and comfort-able.

WORTH

The moment she discov-
ered her worth became the
moment she began to value
herself and let go of anyone
and anything that didn't.
She realized she no longer
wanted anyone to serve a
purpose in her life if they
weren't willing to treat her
the way she deserved, so
she started with the way
she treated herself to set
the tone for what she would
accept going forward.

SEARCHING

I searched for you. I searched for you in people, places, and things. I searched for you in
places I thought I could find you to make me
whole and give me peace again. But I couldn't
find you. In fact, I found nothing, I found
everything but you and realized that instead, I
was in search of something else. I was looking
for the person I lost when you left, and in that
search, I found myself. I have found who I have
been looking for this whole time, the person I
was always meant to be, within all the pieces
that were left behind. I am whole again, and
with that, I have found peace.

When I was on the path of discovery, of finding myself, and thinking that my happiness revolved around others, I searched in other people for the things that were always hidden inside of me. I searched for happiness, joy, and wholeness, and most importantly, I searched for peace. I searched to be completed by other people through the things they were incapable of giving me because those things were inside of me the entire time.

Think about it. How can you give to anyone else something that is missing inside of you? It's not possible. We give a false sense of satisfaction to others, and it's temporary. Yes, you can be happy with someone. Yes, you can even be at peace with someone. And, yes, you can feel complete with someone too. But if you feel none of these things when you're alone, it's a false sense of satisfaction that is fleeting.

For me, it only lasted for moments at a time. It's like the feeling of euphoria. That moment is filled with a lot of excitement and a lot of rushed energy that makes you feel free and liberated, but after a moment, it fades away, and then you have to find it again. You are in search of your next "high." It's the same when it comes to our sense of self and how we truly feel inside. If we are only happy when we are around others, but are unhappy when we're alone, then we are giving others a false sense of happiness where no real satisfaction exists. You are not being authentic and true, and at that point, you are only deceiving yourself.

I no longer wanted to be that person, and I no longer wanted to be at that place. I wanted whatever I had to give going forward to be authentic and true; *I wanted to be seen for who I am.*

Let's face it. We all have something about us that we wouldn't want another person to find out, right? Whether it's something external or internal, we become great pretenders with hiding and burying those things beneath our layers. Frankly, I was tired of that. I mean, how does it feel? I want you to locate and find that thing you hide, and ask yourself how that thing makes you feel. How long will you continue to bury and mask it with something that draws favorable attention? You see, that's it. It doesn't feel good, it doesn't feel right, and no matter how much you try to avoid it, you have to face that you in the mirror—stripped and unmasked—and deal with all the issues you have buried for so long.

It's deeper than your emotional outbursts and even deeper than when you are seeking your next victim to lash out at. It's far greater than the relationships you seek one after the other every time one fails. Whether it's hurt that you still carry from being abandoned, the act of having your innocence taken from you, or not being

"Healing starts at your breaking point."

told that you were enough when you were a child, you have to be willing to trace it back to that thing. I can assure you it will lead to that place where it first began. *Healing starts at your breaking point, so break. Invite healing so that you can discover your true worth, which isn't measured on a scale of what happened to you.*

FINDING MY FOOTING

Readjusting to a new normal was challenging for me, to say the least, but with time, I would adjust to being a single woman. This time, however, I would be more aware of who I am and what I have to offer. After fighting to hold on to a relationship that I desperately wanted to work, I now found myself making personal adjustments, including the choices I made, for the better by raising my standards. I was no longer willing to accept being handed the very least of what someone offered to me or being in a relationship for the sake of passing time or in order to avoid loneliness.

Setting standards and having certain expectations can easily be seen as unrealistic and unobtainable, but the truth is I was tired of getting it wrong—I wanted to get it right. Most importantly, I wanted to get it right by following God's lead. For me, this means making better choices and being clear—starting with myself first, knowing what I needed as opposed to what I wanted or desired and having an awareness of what I was willing and unwilling to accept when the time came to begin dating again.

Primarily, this would mean putting God first and

making Him the center of my entire life—not just pieces of it, like I had done in the past, but all of me. There would be no guarantee that I would always get it right. But I was more aware that if, at any point, being open with someone new meant going against what I know and believe, I would have to quickly close that door and walk away. I was unwilling to stay in a situation that would make me feel uncomfortable or keep me from a place of peace.

I began thinking of God's unconditional love for me and how it felt. I knew through having a relationship with Him what love should and shouldn't feel like. This didn't mean perfection nor that I would live my life with ease, but I had to be aware. I know that God wants what's best for me, as He does for all of us whom He loves. So why would I sacrifice and exchange His perfect will for something less?

Why would I accept less when He wanted more for me? God's best is what's best for me even if that meant Him wanting me to go through a season of being single, requiring me to solely rely on and trust Him. If that is what He wanted for me for the rest of my life so I could live out His purpose, plan and will, then so be it. As hard as it may have been to accept, I gave myself no other choice but to trust Him and know that He had my entire life already mapped out. There would be no need for me to worry or wonder, although it didn't keep me from questioning Him during the most emotional and trying times.

He knows our heart and knows when we are ready. And there have been times I wondered if God had perhaps forgotten about me and whether or not He thought I was worthy enough for the things my heart desired. The truth is He didn't forget me. He knew I wasn't ready for the things my heart longed for regardless of what I had accomplished or the goals I had set and completed. It seemed that every time I reached a pinnacle in my life that was praiseworthy and commendable, and I would say, "Hey, God, I'm ready; task completed," He wanted more. How much more? More than I even expected from myself.

It was clear that God's vision was more in depth and had excellence written all over it, while I was willing to simply arrive at a destination and say OK, I'm good right here.

My good wasn't good enough; He wanted more from me. Not because I knew I was capable of it but because He knew. I had to be willing to listen with an ear to hear and an open heart to receive. Amongst many things, I would have to learn what it meant to love, and

> *"Relaxing your standards or feeling guilty for them leads you into the arms of the wrong person."*

who was worthy to receive the love I have to give. Yes, worthy. After all, didn't we have to be worthy of God's love before receiving it? And once He found us worthy, He gave us His all, didn't He? That was enough assurance for me to face whatever was to come.

Singleness gets lonely; I understand all too well how this feels. However, I will not allow it to make me feel guilty for setting standards and having reasonable expectations from the person who pursues me, and neither should you. *Relaxing your standards or feeling guilty for them leads you into the arms of the wrong person when the wait seems to be a bit longer than you anticipated.* Your expectations should be reasonable and along the lines of what you are willing to give in return. From a woman who is a homemaker to the woman in the executive boardroom, you are all so incredibly worthy!

There is something about you that is unlike anyone else, and *the components of your worth will never be found in someone other than you.* You'll find it hidden in the depths of your heart. This leads me to ask you, what's hidden in your heart? What thoughts and feelings dwell there? Who does that woman you see in the mirror represent, and how does she make you feel when no one's looking? I want you to peel

> *"The components of your worth will never be found in someone other than you."*

back the layers and begin wiping away the make-up, peeling off the lash extensions, taking out the hair extensions, and removing the nail polish. Who do you see? Who's that woman hidden behind it all? Is it your authentic self or who you want others to believe? When you can begin removing all of these things that can easily be used to define you based on what others can see, when you begin cleaning up your insides and removing the filters, that's when you'll begin finding your footing as a woman and your place of belonging in this world. For where your heart is, your treasure is hidden as well. I found my footing and who I am without the masks in God.

INTENTIONAL LOVE

I wanted to ensure that going forward, I was clear about my intentions, so I strove to be pure in everything I did. I was determined and wanted to be intentional with the way I love, who I would love, and whether or not they showed me they were worth my time, attention, and everything I have to offer. More than anything, I vowed to start with myself first. What does being intentional mean to you? What thoughts come to mind, and what evidence do you look for to confirm a person's intentions? If I wanted to know what these things not only felt like and who was going to receive it, I first had to become familiar with how it felt. Sounds a bit funny, right? The truth is, self-care and self-love begin with you.

If you don't treat yourself in a manner that feels good during singleness, how will you know once you begin dating or getting acquainted with someone if how they treat you feels good or bad? And this doesn't just go for love relation-ships but also friendships and associates too. Learning how to love intentionally wasn't going to be easy for me, and although at times it did become very difficult and trying, I started by doing a lot of things alone. I learned a lot about my likes, dislikes, and what it felt like not to have anyone to turn and run to except God. This time alone prepared me to be ready for future relationships. I ate out alone and attended events by myself. I know what you're thinking; she did these things by herself? Did she not have someone she could call and ask to accompany her? There had to be someone, right? Of course there was, but I chose to learn loving intentionally this way.

> "Being intentional gave me a choice and a right to choose."

I discovered so many things about myself without any distractions, suggestions, or recommendations from anyone. I learned to make decisions, stick with them, and follow through. If I wasn't able to understand who I am by myself, gaining a sense of confidence with the thoughts, choices, and decisions I made, how would I have that confidence with someone else? I learned through doing all of these things how to be of one accord.

Being intentional gave me a choice and a right to choose, and it helped me learn how to get a feel for someone and discern better—I became aware. I learned that just because someone may look good or emulate the ideal of what is appealing to my eyes, this didn't mean they were good from their insides or good for me. Even if my intention is good towards someone, it doesn't mean their intentions are the same as mine. Everything started with me, especially if it meant allowing someone to be a part of my life.

If you recall, in a previous chapter, I discussed the importance of guarding and protecting your heart. That is no different than how you love with intention. How you treat yourself will reflect in how you treat others. What you internalize eventually externalizes if you don't address it. We have this idea that we are able to hide and cover who we really are when, in fact, it all begins unfolding with time. And you have to ask yourself, how much of what's broken, damaged, and in need of repair do you want someone else to continually deal with? That's what I want you to confront and ask yourself if your desire is to love intentionally.

It's paramount during times like this to be intentional, upfront, and clear about your desires and expectations to everyone you meet and interact with. It can be a bit nerve-racking having these types of conversations, and sometimes we dance around important topics in fear of scaring the other person away or thinking that we may ruin a good thing if we are honest. But the truth is you won't scare away the person who shares the same morals, beliefs, and standards as you. *Being intentional avoids disappointment and heartbreak and saves time.*

> "You won't scare away the person who shares the same morals, beliefs, and standards as you."

MYSELF

I'd rather be by myself than
be with someone who doesn't
value me and appreciate my
presence. I learned through
experience that it didn't matter
who I was with because it started with me and what I allowed
and was willing to accept—if I
was unwilling to see my worth
and love myself first, then no
one would love me as much
or treat me as worthy as I now
know I deserve.

VALIDATE ME

Validate me, validate me, validate me, please! At one point in my life, I longed to be validated by others with words of affirmation in order for me to feel that what was being said was actually true. Whether it be from hearing a compliment or whatever else, it would get my attention, keep it, and make me feel more sure and confident. It wasn't what I was telling myself or how I felt within, so I needed to hear it from outside. I lacked confidence, and that played a huge role in what I accepted, because when you lack self-confidence, it also affects your self-esteem, causing you to accept less from everyone, including yourself. Unfortunately, it also meant accepting very little effort from someone who wanted all my time and attention. Whatever little was offered, I accepted because it was enough for me since, at that time, I didn't know my complete worth.

Truth be told, I didn't see any of what I heard when I looked in the mirror at myself, as I mentioned before. I didn't see beauty, and I certainly didn't see gorgeous, or for that matter, anything that seemed favorable. Growing up, there were things I felt insecure about, things I wished were different, things I prayed to God about, asking him why. I didn't like my full lips or the fact that I had fine hairs on my arms. I especially didn't like that I had stretch marks on my bottom or the ones that hugged my thighs tightly like a winding road; I saw no beauty in those places. And because that space inside of me had a void, I saw it as a negative. So, whenever a light shone on it, I felt filled and wanted more and more of it.

The thing about feeling you need to be validated by others, not knowing yourself, is that it leaves you emptier, and you continue searching for more of what you are not even sure of. What changed was me not wanting to feel a continuous void, the feeling of loneliness, sadness, and potentially anything that wasn't healthy for me. I knew that in order for my reliance on others to change when it regarded hearing a compliment from them, I needed to start seeing myself as beautiful, pretty, and gorgeous, so that's where I started—I started with me.

I have a confession. In addition to what I shared with you in the chapter entitled My Reflection, I used to avoid looking in the mirror, except for when I was fully clothed just to make sure that my clothes looked the way I wanted them to look and the usual reasons why someone uses a mirror. Other than that, especially when I was unclothed, I never looked directly at myself. Yes, that's how insecure I was. I could

> *"I no longer desired to only look the part, I owed it to myself to live the part."*

almost say that I hated what I saw and frankly didn't want anyone else to see me the way I saw myself. Even in relationships, I was consciously this way, although I never openly shared it and hid it very well. But it showed in my choices and the things that I did. In relationships, I developed the pattern, but I didn't notice it until after this last relationship ended. Shortly afterward, once my healing process began, I found that it wasn't something I wanted to carry into my next relationship if this was God's will for my life.

So, the day came when I stood to face the mirror and began looking at myself, from my full lips to the fine hairs on my body, and instead of filling my mind with self-hate and negativity, I began filling it with self-love. On this quest, I started finding beauty in what I once thought wasn't so beautiful. I invited myself back to who God created me to be, not the person I became, the self I constantly ran from and avoided every chance I could.

Taking those steps wasn't easy. It was challenging. I not only wanted to know what others meant when they said you should love yourself and that self-worth begins with you, I wanted to feel it. I no longer desired to only look the part, I owed it to myself to live the part for real. I wanted to be able to say it to others authentically, and if need be, help them start to see themselves in the same light I saw myself. From that moment on, I vowed never to seek validation or approval from anyone except myself and God. This would mean that no matter what, no one could say anything that would control the way I saw myself. I would always choose me. I closed the door on feeling the need to be validated by others for good.

> *"As long as you have the acceptance of God, you don't need validation from anyone else."*

At one point or another, you may have struggled with the need to be validated and accepted by others, as I did. And you may still be struggling with this even now. However, I want to remind you that as long as you have the acceptance of God, you don't need validation from anyone else. If you could begin to understand how uniquely well-designed and crafted you are, you would no longer seek validation and would work effortlessly to love yourself just as you are. You give power and control over your life to people when you choose to live by their acceptance and validation of you. There is nothing wrong with growth, self-realization, or self-improvement—I encourage it—but if it means being someone you are not and losing your identity for the sake of someone else, I would ask that you re-evaluate that thought and begin to fall deeply in love with yourself.

A BURIED PAST

I buried my past well—a past with unaddressed and suppressed emotions that I hid in the depths of my mind and never openly spoke about or shared with anyone. There were even deeper underlying issues that began to come undone, and things became real. It was time to address them, and I was ready. I realized that I went from the pains of broken- ness in one relationship and entered the one that I was in for many years with unrealistic expectations—expectations that my brokenness could be mended and fixed if I gave it some time. I discovered that was why I remained connected and stayed longer than I was supposed to with people who no longer deserved to be a part of my life. And because I didn't give myself enough time to get the closure I needed and properly heal, those people came through a revolving door that I gave them access to. I didn't know better, so it wasn't until I took the time to unravel and trace back into my past that I discovered and became aware of these things.

A previous relationship had ended prior to the one I was in, but I do not recall at any point giving myself enough time to heal. And to be honest, it wasn't that I didn't give myself enough time but rather that I didn't know time alone was what I needed. Mentally, I was in a place where all I could do was focus on the person I saw externally. I did not give any thought, care, or attention to the person internally or to what needed to take place before I moved on. There I was at that time, a young, naïve, insecure woman who knew very little about herself and not much about the world but desperately longed to be loved. This longing created the very door that I would open and walk through into the next relationship, and it would teach me all I needed to know.

Let's turn the tables a bit because I want to give you a perspective about choice versus reality even when things don't work out the way your heart desires. When you copulate with someone and conceive a child—your heart's desire is to be loved, embraced, and build with this person for the rest of your life. But that's not how my story went. In fact, it went in the opposite direction. I can't begin to tell you how long I struggled with the fact that what I wanted wasn't what I got, and for several years, although I had physically moved on, emotionally, I was still torn and controlled with my feelings in the sense of how it related to this past relationship. It could have been the least of things that were said or done that affected me, and I allowed it; I made that choice. Tied to this prior relationship is a child, a child who will keep me and him connected

> *"Once you allow something or someone to control your emotions, it will dictate your actions."*

for the remainder of our lives. What helped me realize how much control and power I gave him over my life was where I would find myself every time my expectations of him didn't match my reality. One day, I found myself crying, tears streaming down my face like an unguarded floodgate, and I was emotional because I was hurt over something he had said to me.

It was in that moment where, having found myself there far too many times before, I had to stop and realize a few things about this situation. One, I was allowing someone I was no longer physically with but was still connected to by a child, to have access to my emotions. Second, my peace was being disturbed, and I was not being who God created me to be as a mother to our child because I was no longer in control of my feelings and had given that power to him. Lastly, but most importantly, I realized it was time to stop giving this person whose relationship with me had ended some time ago, continuous control over my life. It was time to break this cycle and erupt this destructive pattern. What an epiphany that was for me! Control over my life? No way. How? *Once you allow something or someone to control your emotions, it will dictate your actions and how you live out your life.*

From that moment on, there were times when, emotionally, I was tried and tempted relentlessly, but I chose to stop responding and reacting to familiarity. His expectation was to get the same response and reaction that I used to give. Instead, I chose to respond with love, kindness, and without an emotional reaction that would cause me to act out of character with the woman I vowed peace with—myself. Who would have thought that responding with love would be the remedy necessary to avoid any more hurt or pain in an area of my life where there had been nothing but hurt and pain at one point? That's the difference when you choose to stop feeding your pain and instead respond with love—God's love, the same love that isn't biased, isn't puffed up, and forgives all, even when you don't get the apology you deserve. It may not change the other person internally; however, it can change how you are approached and treated going forward. A level of respect is formed simply because you chose love. Similar to soul ties, issues from your past can arise when unaddressed. You will find yourself wondering, "Why does this same thing that I left behind so long ago continue to occur over and over again?"

A soul tie binds two souls together in the spiritual realm. Being connected, and remaining attached to someone you are not married to, can continuously attract you to someone you are not supposed to be with. For example, a woman with low self-esteem can attract a man who feeds her emotional desires and longing to hear all the things she wants to hear. Yet she is desperately at a place where she needs to love herself first in order to be loved completely and wholly, as an aware woman, in the best way. Being this vulnerable leads to the manipulation of your mind and emotions when underlying issues from your past are not addressed. Connections are formed through having close relationships, including by making commitments, vows, and agreements, otherwise known as promises; and also by sexual intimacy. When it comes to forming connections, moreoften than not, sexual intimacy takes the lead.

Unless you slow down long enough to notice this, or it's pointed out to you, this cycle will repeat itself and continue. This is why giving yourself enough time to figure things out after a break-up or separation is vital.

It's easy to unknowingly walk around carrying the brokenness, pain, and weight from your past. Some of it, you may be ashamed to face and deal with, while other parts of it, you've yet to realize the effect that has continued to take place. The wounds you have cry out—yet still go unnoticed and unaddressed time after time. I buried that part of my past without healing and closure, only to move forward without there being an end. Where there was supposed to be a period, there were commas.

This is why carrying hurt and pain that hasn't been resolved can affect everything when you try to move forward. You unintentionally carry baggage. Baggage full of heartbreak, brokenness, abuse, sadness, depression, stress, anxiety, worry, you name it, it happens. Especially when you don't know your worth and didn't take the time to properly heal and face these things one by one. For most of us, everything won't heal all at once, and most times, you'll walk around unaware of your gaping wounds. It takes dedication and it takes time. There will be parts of yourself you will immediately recognize need addressing, while other things are revealed to you over time and through different experiences. However, once you become aware, you become responsible.

GROWING PAINS

As I transitioned more into my adult life; I found how extremely important it became to take time to explore and get to know myself, even in the midst of others and being a part of their lives. Here's a hard truth that many shy away from or don't want to face: You will outgrow people along the way. I know, I know; letting go is never easy, and it won't always be, but you have to be willing to face that truth and grow even you're not ready. So, yes, this means even after heartbreak, disappointment, a setback, or brokenness, you have to gather enough strength to continue moving forward.

Things change suddenly, or even in an instant, when a relationship or friendship ends. But somehow, we've become so accustomed to how things are that we don't realize the subtle changes that are taking place around us and within beforehand. Change takes place beneath the surface and cannot be seen until the stages of transformation begin. So, once it's time to make the decision to leave a relationship or to part ways with someone for one reason or another, a shift begins to take place similar to how growth occurs. Outgrowing a relationship won't always be because the other person is bad or toxic, but may be solely because you are both growing but in different directions. Relationships are difficult to move forward from for several reasons.

> "After heartbreak, memories linger for some time."

After heartbreak, memories linger for some time, and letting go of history or the idea of who you thought someone was when you first met them or who they should be can be disappointing.

Think about a seed when it is planted; its purpose is to grow. It is meant to not only grow and push through but, in its final transition, it is meant to bloom. That may have been one of the hardest parts of my growth to accept. Regardless of how I felt about parting ways with people I loved and cared about deeply, God desired something else for me, and it required a shift in my growth. Grow even while I was in pain. Grow when all I wanted to do was hold on and cry. Grow when the last thing I wanted to do was face everything that I avoided as I experienced heartbreak. Yes, grow.

I began to take a closer look at a flower and how beautiful it is once it comes into full bloom, otherwise known as seed spreading. But I never thought about its process or what it had to go through to get there. In order to under-stand its final stage, I took a look at the many stages it has to undergo and used it as a metaphor for what took place during the period of my growth.

The beginning stage of the flower is called the seed, followed by germination, growth, reproduction, pollination, and seed spreading, its final stage.

Imagine yourself as a flower and the process you have gone through to become who you are this very moment. It wasn't easy, was it? But first, you had to be planted. You started off as a seed, which can also be seen as your time of isolation. During this time of isolation, you began to experi-ence different things in your life, which is the next process, called germination. That was the moment your environment became uncomfortable. You began to learn new things and began shifting, searching for a place to be rooted and grounded, looking for something to sustain you that would be able to invite and welcome the person you had started to become for the better. At that point, you are ready to outgrow who you were before, including the people, places, things,

and environments that could no longer contain you. Following that is your reproduction stage, pollination, and lastly,
seed spreading. That's when you bloomed!

*"I didn't want
to cling to what
was familiar
knowing that
there was
something
greater for me."*

More than anything, growth begins
with you just as it did for me. It was time
for me to grow, and although it was
uncomfortable, it was necessary. So,
what do you say? Are you ready to grow?
Do you feel it is time for you to bloom,
too? My heart hopes you said yes! Because you shouldn't
allow where you are, even if you find yourself there more
than once, to hold you back or stop you from getting where
you are headed. Your greatest fight becomes your strongest
testimony for someone else, who is waiting on it to help set
them free, just like you. Just like you, they want to bloom!
That's what kept me going; that's why I stayed persistent. I
didn't want to cling to what was familiar knowing that there
was something greater for me and that so much more was
inside of me. I am thankful for my growing pains, and you
shouldn't take lightly the strides you have made as you shift
through your very own growing pains. Change is inevitable;
embrace it.

REJECTIONS RESIDUE

For several years, I dealt with the fear of abandonment, and from time to time, I still do. This fear stemmed from rejection and promise after promise being broken countless times by people I had trusted. Promises that made me feel comfortable enough to give the very best parts of myself, with no regret and nothing to worry about. Yet still, those promises were not kept. That those promises had been broken is what broke me. Not only did I become fearful, but I became very guarded and cautious about how much of myself I would give to anyone, no matter how purposeful or intentional they were.

Rejection hurts, and it leaves a gaping wound that cries for attention. You begin asking yourself what is wrong with you. You ask, why am I not loved and accepted for who I am? Why isn't my enough, enough? I pondered these questions as they swirled through my mind like wind shuffling through leaves. I quickly became defensive every time I met someone, and I wanted to know everything about them immediately, like having an instruction manual for the things I needed to know. I wanted to know what my risks were and what chances I was taking if I didn't follow the written instructions.

Would this person, if I allowed them in, fail me if I didn't follow this guide line by line? You cannot avoid rejection, nor can you remain in hiding, awaiting and praying that you are not abandoned by someone who chooses not to stay.

> *"Rejection carries a residue, which leaves behind a trail."*

I'm sure you have heard the words, "I will never leave you," "I will always be here for you," "I'm not going anywhere," "You can always count on me," just to name a few. In that same thought, I am certain you can also remember how many times those words or commitments were not kept. I quickly came to realize that not only was I was putting more trust in a person than I was in God, but I was also unfairly using past experiences and hurt to keep people out of my life, people who might have meant only good things for me.

The fear of being alone and abandoned can leave you feeling desperate—creating a cycle and pattern of having the need and desire for someone to always be there. The result of someone leaving you can feel like rejection, and the more you are rejected, the more you will search to be accepted by others rather than accepting yourself first. You will search for things to fill that voided area. *Rejection carries a residue, which leaves behind a trail after its first occurrence and will have you searching for things outside of yourself that are within.* I can share from my own personal experience that the only One who will never abandon or reject you is God our Heavenly Father. You can count on Him, and Deuteronomy 31:6 reassures us that He will never leave or forsake us. This is true. No matter who may come or go, you can rest assured that God will be there.

It's easy to accumulate void fillers through having different friendships, associations, and even love relationships that will fill that space so you'll never feel alone. But if none of those people are adding value to you, or vice versa, you'll be in the same place where they found you. When you are afraid to be left by someone, you will also find yourself clinging and holding on to what is unhealthy. I didn't want to be that person, but can't help but remember the times I have found myself there. I had to take accountability and stop allowing myself to self-destruct every time things didn't go how I'd imagine they would.

How do you get through and overcome rejections residue or the fear of abandonment? Is there a practical and effective way? Well, I questioned if it were at all possible and whether or not I would finally overcome this fear. What if I told you that God would orchestrate an intentional abandonment in order for you to receive better, would you agree with me and welcome it, or would you oppose? The most pivotal lesson that I learned about being abandoned is that there were times when I gave more than I was receiving, and unfortunately, nowhere is it written that how we give of ourselves to others should be measured by how much they give us. However, when we hold on to our will for the future, while just around the corner is a better one predestined by God, I believe He will allow those things to take place—especially when it concerns your destiny. It's true that I can have a vision and plan for my life. I can even have a solid goal in place that has been effectively working for some time, but no matter how well put together those goals are or how they may be working out, it doesn't mean they will lead to the destination I have in mind. So, in fact, I can cope with and help manage that fear, but if it means that God wants that person removed from my life, I have no control over that and cannot stop a separation or parting from taking place.

KNOWING THE DIFFERENCE

All women have a little girl hidden inside of them. A girl who longs to be loved in the way her father loved her when she was a child. She not only longs to be loved and cared for, but she wants to be protected and feel safe, too. When a woman lets her guard down and opens up her heart to love, she desires an unconditional and pure love. Yes, action speaks! It speaks louder than any whispering word. Commitment and following through from start to finish helps eliminate doubt and fear from the heart of a woman. No woman grows out of being that little girl and having a desire to be loved in the way her father loves her. I want a man with integrity, moral, and character. I want to be loved privately in the same way it's displayed publicly. Confidence attracts and keeps the attention of two people, but it's important that the relationship is centered in God. A man's relationship should be connected to God, or he must at least have an understanding of who he is. This is where the foundation is laid in order for him to begin building.

Every man's growth to maturity is different and it happens at different stages in his life. Men are intentional, and I had to learn the difference between who was intentional, and who was just looking for a good time. Knowing what I want and desire sets the stage for who I will give my time and attention to. This was invaluable and important for me to know. I believe that a boy who is led by a man will become a man when it is time. But I also believe that even when he is led, it doesn't mean that he will be a man who leads when it's time, and this can be a bit frustrating. When a man has an intent to pursue a woman, he will pursue her. This makes him intentional. Knowing who you are as a woman invites the kind of men you will either allow to be a part of your life or not. The love you have for yourself, knowing your worth and being aware of your value, sets the table for whom you will allow to feast at it.

I have had expectations concerning the maturity of men, and I have been disappointed, not realizing how much room for growth he still has, and that it is entirely up to him to answer that call hidden within. Whether he embodies the role God designed and created him for, or he pursues being who he has always wanted to be, it's entirely his choice.

I have personally grown a lot, and during every stage,

when it was time for me to grow, I went through a pruning process where it was cycles of my time to become and embrace or my time to let go and transform. It was all a matter of me not wanting to remain the same if it meant effective growth.

To me, a man is more than his looks. He is his character, he is what he says, but most importantly, he is what he does. A man shows you who he is through his integrity, his ambition, and how he represents when no one is looking. A man shows you his strength and courage when he allows himself to be vulnerable. To me, a man is one who is able to love a woman in a way she has never been loved.

You should not only be seen for who you are from the outside. There should be an inclination inside the person who pursues you that yearns to know what else you have to offer that the eye cannot see. When you rush the process of getting to know someone, you can undoubtedly find yourself in a world of pain, disappointment, and heartbreak, leaving you lost and broken. As humans, we naturally have the tendency to overlook, disregard, and even dismiss what we know to be the truth, and that's when we end up further away from our initial intent and purpose. You are not a road map; therefore, it is OK to slow down! You should not have to go from person to person to determine what your future holds concerning a relationship.

> *"You are not a road map; therefore, it is OK to slow down!"*

Before sharing yourself with someone, bear in mind *that who you are connected to can alter the direction of your destiny, and knowing this will help you be vigilant in the decisions you make.* It's entirely up to you to choose. Even while dating and getting to know someone, you shouldn't be afraid to voice your concerns or why you find it challenging to commit to things you may not always agree upon, whether it is out of the way of the Lord and incongruent with your beliefs or outside of your standards and morals. In that same respect, it's important to remain open and teachable while applying understanding in all things. Yes, I said all things. *Communication takes an undying effort to not only hear what the other person is saying but to, most importantly, listen to their heart.*

It can be easy to mistakenly believe that often, women are unwilling to be led by a man or that she intentionally chooses not to be led; however, I find this to be untrue. In fact, a woman is not afraid to follow the lead of a man, but she wants to be sure and confident that he is a man with direction and, most importantly, a man directed by God, based on her values and beliefs. I believe that a woman can be a woman, and be everything God has called and designed her to be, without taking anything away from the man she stands beside. A woman can be confident and bold, dominate in her career, have a strong influence and be influential, and leave a memorable impression amongst those whose presence she graces, and this still will not take away from the man who she stands beside. But these very same characteristics shouldn't be mistaken as her being overly self-reliant or too independent. A man wants to feel secure in who he is, and so does a woman—leaving no room for insecurity, doubt, or lack of belief in who they are individually.

As I consider and think about my own personal desires and prayer, I know it is to marry a man of God, and not one who only speaks it from his mouth, but one who lives it. This assures me that he understands leadership and the importance of leading, but it also tells me that he will be able to acknowledge my strengths with admiration and without fear or intimidation. Not only will he be able to acknowledge my strengths but he will protect and guard the areas of my life that may be weak as if they are his own weaknesses. When he knows a woman of worth is in his presence, a woman who can add to him, he also understands that he has found his strength. Follow-through is invaluable and important to me; it's an indicator that captures and grabs my attention. When a man commits himself and all of his ways to God, a woman will never hesitate to do the same and allow that man to lead her. That's how I know the difference.

YOU HAVE ARRIVED

You have arrived, and upon your arrival, I pray that you have already begun to allow God to mend your brokenness. I pray that you have been compelled to develop a deeper relationship with Him, one that is not only conducive to a better you but one conducive to a you that you can feel proud of. I pray that now your continual picking at your every *wound, bruise, scar, or scab* will stop and you will invite complete healing and restoration. It's time for your transformation to begin, as mine did.

I find you to be *brave, bold, and beautiful* for taking this walk with me, which makes you a conqueror! I hope that you have found the peace your heart has longed for and that your desires will begin to manifest. It is my heart's desire that you will seek the things that bring you joy and that when you find this joy, you will pass this book on to another soul whose heart longs for the very same.

I want your brokenness to be mended and for you to be made emotionally whole. I no longer want you searching relentlessly for pieces from your past that are gone when your future has a reservation with your name on it, patiently waiting for you to say *I AM HERE*. Your past has no bearing on your future. You are *incomparable* and *cannot be labeled, defined,* or *categorized* by who you were or what others have tried to *marginalize* you as. It is time to exchange your ashes for beauty, remove your mask of shame, and thrive in your light and fullness.

As I wrote each and every word, I wanted to give you a sense of my vulnerability and transparency—to feel what I felt. I wanted you to know that you are not alone—you were never alone, and you aren't the only one who has felt *rejected, abandoned* and have faced *heartbreak* or *disappointment.*

You are courageous, and I pray you have found your very own courage to turn the pages, begin again, and find your voice as I did.

ACKNOWLEDGEMENTS

To God, whom I honor and appreciate for seeing in me all the things I never saw in myself. For being patient enough to wait for me to get it together. For loving me in my brokenness until You healed and made me whole again. For always calling me back to You every time I wandered off and got lost, time and time again. For finding me worthy enough and lovable through my pain during the times I found myself unworthy and unlovable. I thank You!

To my son, Boaz: you are a gift that is as irreplaceable as a once-in-a-lifetime opportunity to have a full life. You chose me at a time that I didn't know I would need you the most, and you helped order my steps and the decisions I would make. God knew we would do well together, and for that, there will never be enough ways that I could repay Him than to make sure I give you the life you deserve until you're old enough to live the life of your dreams. For every word of encouragement, kiss, hug, act of kindness or thoughtfulness. For the patience and understanding you extended as I wrote this book, as you were still able to maintain being exceptional and excel in everything you do, I thank you. I stand in awe that God chose me and look forward to who you will become as you continue to grow.

To my parents, Cecil and Iris Williams, who I could never repay for the sacrifices you both equally made. Thank you for introducing me to Christ at an early age and always reinforcing that without Him, I could never be who I am today. Thank you for raising me with principles, morals, and values and for teaching me the importance of loving with my whole heart. For teaching me the importance of loving people and accepting them for where they are and not my expectations. Thank you for standing in love together for over thirty-six years and being to each other what you both needed in order to be to me what I needed. My beloved mother, Iris, although you are no longer with us here on Earth, I honor and acknowledge you as though you still were. Because of you, I am.

To my brothers, Joel and Shurwayne, who are equally as caring as they are loving. Joel, you continually keep me motivated, aware, and filled with life, while Shurwayne, you keep me sharp and on my toes. You never gave me room to settle and always encouraged me to take the road less traveled.

Thank you both for allowing me to be myself by loving me with your all and accepting who I am in my fullness, even when I may have gotten intense. You both understand how passionate I am and have accepted it with open arms.

To Dwayne Dillion, a loyalist and friend who is not only irreplaceable and rare but one of only a handful God made that way. You are a friend who is always diligent enough to listen, patient enough to understand, and caring enough to share your wisdom and encourage me every time I felt I had no more to give, and staying until I had enough strength to continue on my own.

To my Pastor, Damion Archat, thank you for pouring into me message after message, time and time again. Words cannot express how grateful I am that God strategically placed you into my life to be my leader at such a time as this! Just a few years ago, at a time when I was broken, you told me this would happen before I knew it would, and now it has; the story has been written. Thank you for not being selfish, but selfless and for being God's servant and vessel.

To Curtrice Williams, the one God allowed to come into my life when I needed you the most. Thank you for allowing God to use you as you told me what I needed to hear when He directed you to speak life into me. Thank you for telling me I could do this and finish and for not allowing fear or doubt to hold you back, but propel you in the direction God has for your life.

To Alex Jeanty, the one I reached out to first when I was ready to start sharing publicly what I had written privately. Thank you for your guidance and always being honest with me when it was needed, tough on me when I would soften up, but still knowing how to keep me going with your jokes and accepting me for who I am with all my quirkiness. For understanding at my level and knowing that at times I needed a little bit more than a simple or quick answer.

To you—yes, you—for allowing me into your heart and the crevices of your soul, inhaling me like a breath of fresh air. I thank you.

A NOTE FROM THE AUTHOR

When I first sat down to write my story, I wrote it with you in my heart. I wanted to share my personal story because it's one that many can relate to, but few have heard. As women, it's sometimes difficult to find the courage to let our guard down and unmask our shame. Over time, I no longer felt the need to wear this mask of shame, but instead, I was compelled to remove it and help remind someone, someone just like you, how worthy and precious you are, and that no matter what, you still have a fighting chance because you have survived all of the things that were meant to bring you down. For me, it has been a long time coming, and it came with so many obstacles, setbacks, and disappointments. But I am so glad that I got the opportunity to share this part of my heart with you. From my heart to yours, thank you for inviting me into your heart, a heart that will always be safe with me.

With love,

Priscilla

AUTHOR'S BIOGRAPHY

Priscilla P. Williams is a devoted mother, an art lover, a creative being, an avid reader, and a writer on a mission to restore to wholeness women who are enduring the storm of emotional devastation.

Priscilla is passionate about women becoming vulnerable enough to discuss their feelings of brokenness and unworthiness and about proving to them that they're highly valued and deserving of love. She hopes to encourage women to revel in their true identities by cultivating confidence in what makes them unique.

Priscilla is unashamed of her relationship and love for God and His ability to transform lives as He did hers. She believes that with a willing heart of surrender that no one has to remain at the place where brokenness left them, but that they can be transformed simply by saying, *yes*.

Priscilla can often be found spending time with her family, friends, and other loved ones. She is a fan of books, documentaries, and street art, and she loves finding new restaurants or other undiscovered locations. Priscilla currently resides in the South Florida area.

Here's how you can connect with Priscilla

Instagram: @herheartwritesopenly

Facebook: www.facebook.com/herheartwritesopenly

For booking and speaking engagements e-mail:
herheartwritesopenly@gmail.com

Printed in Great Britain
by Amazon